Saint Bernadette
and the Miracles of Lourdes

My soul proclaims the greatness of the Lord,
my spirit rejoices in God my Savior
for he has looked with favor on his lowly servant.

Magnificat, Luke 1:47-48

.

Saint Bernadette
and the Miracles of Lourdes

Written and Illustrated by
Demi

MAGNIFICAT · Ignatius

In Lourdes, France, in the foothills of the mountains, there lived a miller and his wife. François and Louise Soubirous were kind and hard-working people. Their first child, a daughter, was born on January 7, 1844. They named her Marie Bernarde, but everyone called her Bernadette.

When Bernadette was a baby, her mother had an accident and could not take care of her. So a good woman in a nearby village nursed her for a while. What joy when the family was at last reunited! Soon afterward, Bernadette's sister Toinette was born.

When Bernadette was ten years old, her parents lost their mill. They both went out to work for other people, but they could not support their growing family. They had to send back Bernadette to the woman who had nursed her.

Bernadette tended the woman's sheep. She did not know how to read or write because she had never been to school. But she knew how to pray. She knew the Our Father and the Hail Mary, and she always had a rosary in her pocket.

Bernadette dearly wanted to learn from the nuns in Lourdes and to make her First Communion there, and she was homesick. So the fourteen-year-old said a fond farewell to her foster mother and walked home.

Her family was now very poor, and they lived in a small room that had been used as a jail. It was rundown, cold, and damp. Bernadette was often sick, but she was always cheerful. When she was not in school, she helped her mother at home.

On February 11, 1858, Bernadette went to the river with her sister Toinette and their friend Jeanne to collect firewood. When they reached a millstream, Toinette and Jeanne kicked off their wooden shoes and ran across. They cried out because the water was very cold.

After she took off her shoes and one sock, Bernadette heard a noise like a gust of wind. But–how strange– when she looked about she saw that the trees were not swaying in any wind. Taking off her second sock, she heard the noise again. This time when she raised her head, she saw a beautiful lady in a nearby cave, or grotto.

Around the lady was a gentle white light. She was wearing a white dress with a blue sash and a long white veil. On top of each bare foot was a yellow rose. A long rosary hung over her arm.

Bernadette felt a little scared. So she pulled the rosary out of her pocket. As she made the Sign of the Cross, her fear disappeared.

Bernadette prayed the rosary, and the lady seemed to follow along by passing her beads through her fingers. She said nothing but the Glory Be after each decade. After the rosary, the lady motioned to Bernadette to come closer, but Bernadette did not dare. The lady then smiled at her and vanished. When the other girls came back with armloads of wood, Bernadette was still on her knees. They laughed at her and then scolded her for not helping them.

On the way home, Toinette asked Bernadette if something had frightened her. Bernadette told her about the lady, begging her not to tell anyone. But that same evening, Toinette told their mother everything Bernadette had said. Worried for Bernadette, their mother told them to stay away from the grotto.

A few days later, Bernadette felt drawn to the grotto. She begged her parents to let her go there with some friends, and they finally agreed.

At the grotto, the lady appeared again. Bernadette sprinkled holy water on the vision, and the lady smiled. The other children did not see the lady, but they saw that Bernadette's face was shining.

Bernadette's parents did not know what to think. None of their relatives and none of the nuns teaching Bernadette believed her story. Rumors spread that Bernadette was either lying or crazy.

Two wealthy women who thought Bernadette might be telling the truth went with her to the grotto. When the lady appeared, Bernadette asked her to write her name on a piece of paper. The lady smiled and said she did not need to write anything. She asked Bernadette to meet with her for fourteen days. She said that she did not promise to make Bernadette happy in this life, but in the next.

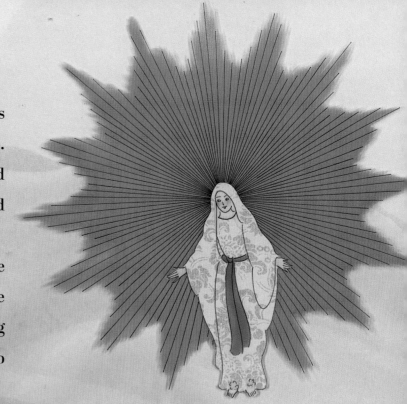

The next day, eight people, including Bernadette's mother and aunt, followed the girl to the grotto. She carried a lighted blessed candle. Again she prayed with the lady, who was silent. The same thing happened the following day.

On Sunday, February 21, a doctor joined the hundred people who went with Bernadette to the grotto. He felt her pulse and checked her breathing as she prayed. Meanwhile, the lady told Bernadette to pray to God for sinners.

Later, a town official questioned Bernadette. He thought the girl was sincere but crazy. Then a police officer told her she was causing trouble for everyone and must stay away from the grotto.

But Bernadette could not stay away. She visited the grotto on February 23, and one hundred fifty people went with her.

The next day there were twice as many people at the grotto. The lady again asked Bernadette to pray for sinners. She asked the girl to kiss the ground for the conversion of sinners, and Bernadette did as she asked.

On Thursday, February 25, three hundred people were with Bernadette as she prayed. Suddenly, she began acting very strangely.

The lady told Bernadette to drink from the spring. Not seeing a spring, the girl walked toward the river. The lady called her back and pointed to a little pool of dirty water. As Bernadette scratched in it, more water came, but it was muddy when she tried to drink it.

Next, the lady told Bernadette to eat the herbs beside the spring. Bernadette saw only grass, so she pulled it up and ate it. The people watching her thought the poor girl was crazy.

But she was not crazy. The pool of water grew and grew. It was a spring, just as the lady had said. A week later, it was pouring forth twenty-five thousand gallons of water every twenty-four hours, as it still does to this day.

On Saturday, February 27, eight hundred people gathered at the grotto. The lady was silent, but Bernadett[e] prayed as before and drank from the growing spring. The following day, more than a thousand people arrived[.] Again Bernadette knelt and kissed the ground as she prayed for sinners. This time some of the people imitated he[r.]

The town officials were worried about the safety of so many people. A judge told Bernadette that sooner or later someone would get hurt. If she went back to the grotto, he warned, he would put her in jail.

But Bernadette insisted that she must keep going to the grotto until the following Thursday because she had promised to meet with the lady for fourteen days.

Bernadette went to the grotto the very next day. It was Monday, March 1, and fifteen hundred people had come to see what would happen.

For the first time, a priest was there, and he was moved by what he saw. As Bernadette began the rosary, she looked like any other girl. Then suddenly, she gleamed as if she were in heaven. She acted as though she were talking with a real person. After an hour, she kissed the ground and stood up.

That night, a woman who had hurt her arm by falling out of a tree went to the grotto. She bathed her arm in the water of the spring, and when she took it out, she was healed.

There were other miracles in the early days of that spring. A man had lost the vision in his right eye in a mining accident. After rubbing his eye with the spring water, he was able to see again. A woman brought her dying baby to the grotto. She put the child in the water, and he was healed too.

News of the first miracle spread like wildfire. The next day, even more people went to the grotto. The lady asked Bernadette to tell the priests of Lourdes to lead a procession to the grotto and to build a chapel there.

Bernadette went to Father Peyramale, the parish priest, and told him what the lady had said. The priest wanted to believe the girl, but he needed proof that the lady was sent by God. He said that he would not obey the lady until he knew her name.

The next day, Bernadette went to the grotto at 7 o'clock in the morning. She was followed by three thousand people. Bernadette had planned to ask the lady her name, but she did not appear.

After school, Bernadette felt very strongly that she should go back to the grotto. This time the lady appeared. When the girl asked for her name, the lady only smiled.

Thursday, March 4, was the fourteenth day since the lady had first spoken to Bernadette. About eight thousand people went to the grotto. They were expecting the lady to say her name, but she did not.

For the next twenty days, Bernadette stayed away from the grotto. Then on Thursday, March 25, she felt the need to pray there again.

Thousands of people were at the grotto when the lady appeared. And when Bernadette again asked for her name, the lady lifted her eyes to heaven, joined her hands, and said, "I am the Immaculate Conception."

These were the last words she spoke to Bernadette.

Bernadette ran to the parish church. Over and over, she repeated the lady's strange words so that she would not forget them. When she found Father Peyramale, she told him what the lady had said. The priest was astounded and asked Bernadette if she knew what the words meant. She said no.

The girl did not know that four years earlier the pope had declared the Church's belief in the Immaculate Conception, which means God created Mary full of grace so that she could be the Mother of Jesus. The beautiful lady was none other than the Blessed Virgin!

The lady appeared again on Wednesday, April 7. It was a very windy day, and Bernadette cupped her right hand around the flame of her candle so that it would not go out.

The thousands of witnesses who saw the flame licking her hand were sure that she would be badly burned. Yet when a doctor examined her hand, it was unharmed.

The last apparition at the grotto happened on Thursday, July 16. Bernadette went there to pray, but her way was blocked by a police barrier. Yet she saw the lady from the far side of the river. She was more beautiful than ever.

People from far and wide came to Lourdes. They wanted to pray at
the grotto and bathe in the spring. And they wanted to see Bernadette.
Even the wife of the French emperor was interested in Lourdes.

Bernadette did not want all of this attention. She wanted only to live in peace. To do this, she moved in with the nuns who had taught her. She helped them to care for the sick in their hospice.

The people who came to Lourdes still wanted to meet Bernadette. So in 1866, at the age of twenty-two, Bernadette went to the sisters' motherhouse in Nevers. There she became a nun. She took the veil and the name Sister Marie-Bernarde.

The move was very hard on Bernadette. She had never been so far away from home, and she missed her family very much. After a few months, she was very sick. When she got better, her job was to care for the sisters when they were ill. Everyone could see how kind and gentle she was.

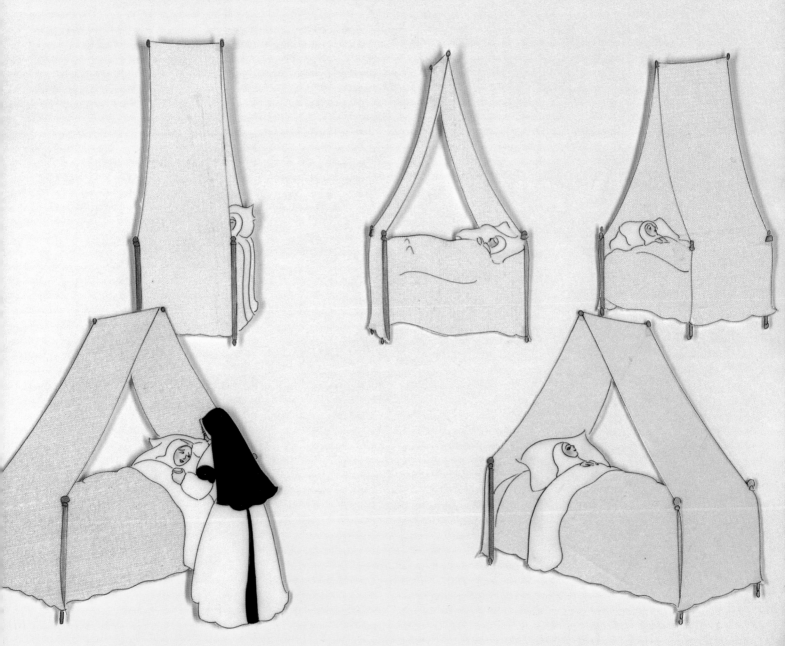

As the years passed, other health problems arose. Bernadette became weaker and weaker. She died on Easter Monday, April 14, 1879, while holding a crucifix in her hand and asking Mary to pray for her, a sinner. She was only thirty-five years old.

To the Queen of Heaven, Bernadette wrote in her journal, How happy my soul was, good Mother, when I had the good fortune to gaze upon you! How I love to recall the pleasant moments spent under your gaze, so full of kindness and mercy for us. Yes, tender Mother, you stooped down to earth to appear to a mere child. You, the Queen of Heaven and earth, deigned to make use of the most fragile being in the world's eyes.

Many people believed that Bernadette was a saint. And on December 8, 1933, Pope Pius XI made it official.

Saint Bernadette's feast day is April 16, and she is the patron saint of the sick, the poor, martyrs, shepherds, and shepherdesses. She is also the patron of Lourdes, France.

Today Lourdes is one of the world's most important Catholic shrines. More than six million visitors from all the ends of the earth go there each year. They pray in the magnificent chapel, bathe in the spring water, and join in candlelight processions. Everything that the Mother of Jesus requested has been fulfilled.

Since the apparitions, about seven thousand visitors to Lourdes have experienced unexplained cures. Sixty-nine cases have been officially recognized as miraculous. These are proven physical healings that science cannot explain. Other healings, mostly spiritual, have been claimed by thousands of people who have visited the place where the Mother of Jesus appeared to Saint Bernadette.

O Virgin Mary,
Christians pray to you in Lourdes,
Ave Maria, hail to you, Mary.

In your sanctuary, refuge of sinners,
hear the cry of your children's hearts!
Ave Maria, hail to you, Mary.

Like Bernadette, I pray
for the salvation of my brothers and sisters.
Ave Maria, hail to you, Mary.

In my heart, O Queen of Heaven,
replace hatred with charity.
Ave Maria, hail to you, Mary.

Tender mother, this is my desire:
to love you on earth and to see you in heaven!
Ave Maria, hail to you, Mary.

(Based on the Lourdes *Ave Maria*)

Under the direction of Romain Lizé, Vice President, MAGNIFICAT
Editor, MAGNIFICAT: Isabelle Galmiche
Editor, Ignatius: Vivian Dudro
Proofreader: Janet Chevrier
Assistant to the Editor: Pascale van de Walle
Layout Designer: Magali Meunier
Production: Thierry Dubus, Sabine Marioni

Printed in July 2017 by TWP, Malaysia
Job number MGN 17021
Printed in compliance with the Consumer Protection Safety Act, 2008.